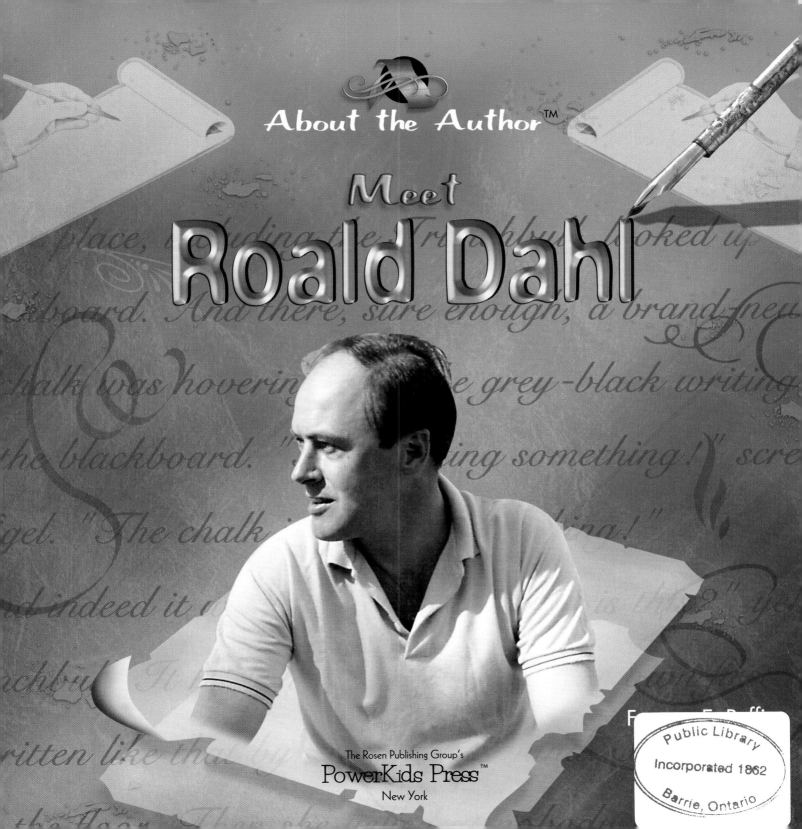

About the Author™

Meet

Roald Dahl

The Rosen Publishing Group's
PowerKids Press™
New York

To the next generation: James, Beth, Davey, Jason, Tim, Justin, Matt, and Paul

Published in 2006 by The Rosen Publishing Group, Inc.
29 East 21st Street, New York, NY 10010

First Edition

Editor: Rachel O'Connor
Book Design: Julio A. Gil
Photo Researcher: Cindy Reiman

Photo Credits: p. 4 © Time Life Pictures/Getty Images; p. 15 © Museum of Flight/Corbis; p. 19 © Getty Images; all other photos, pp. 8 (postcard), 15 (article) © Roald Dahl Nominee Limited; p. 22 (interview) From 'The Author's Eye' © The Roald Dahl Museum and Story Centre/Partners in Health. Directed by Todd McCormick, produced by IMG, 1988.

Grateful acknowledgement is made for permission to reprint previously published material:
p. 5 From CHARLIE AND THE CHOCOLATE FACTORY by Roald Dahl, text copyright © 1964, renewed 1992 by Roald Dahl Nominee Limited. Used by permission of Alfred A. Knopf, an imprint of Random House Children's Books, a division of Random House, Inc.
p. 18 Illustration by Lane Smith, copyright © 1996 by Lane Smith, from JAMES AND THE GIANT PEACH by Roald Dahl, copyright © 1961, renewed 1989 by Roald Dahl. Used by permission of Alfred A. Knopf, an imprint of Random House Children's Books, a division of Random House, Inc.
pp. 20, 21 From MATILDA by Roald Dahl, illustrated by Quentin Blake, copyright © 1988 by Quentin Blake, illustrations. Used by permission of Puffin Books, A Division of Penguin Young Readers Group, A Member of Penguin Group (USA) Inc., 345 Hudson Street, New York, NY 10014. All rights reserved.
p. 21 From MATILDA by Roald Dahl, copyright © 1988 by Roald Dahl, text. Used by permission of Puffin Books, A Division of Penguin Young Readers Group, A Member of Penguin Group (USA) Inc., 345 Hudson Street, New York, NY 10014. All rights reserved.

Library of Congress Cataloging-in-Publication Data

Ruffin, Frances E.
  Meet Roald Dahl / Frances E. Ruffin.
      p. cm. — (About the author)
  Includes index.
  ISBN 1-4042-3134-X (lib. bdg.)
 1. Dahl, Roald—Juvenile literature. 2. Authors, English—20th century—Biography—Juvenile literature. 3. Children's stories—Authorship—Juvenile literature. I. Title. II. Series.
  PR6054.A35Z86 2006
  823'.914—dc22

                                    2005007017

Manufactured in the United States of America

Contents

Roald is pictured here with his son in 1965. Four years earlier Roald had written the very popular children's book James and the Giant Peach. He wrote it for his children.

Modern-day Fairy Tales

Roald (ROO-ahl) Dahl has been described as a teller of modern-day fairy tales. Just as fairy tales have a scary side, so too do Roald's stories for adults and children. Roald often wrote about imaginary creatures. In his book *The BFG*, Roald wrote about Giant Country, which is a land filled with people-eating giants. In *The Witches*, witches never spit because they might show their blue saliva. Roald also wrote about bratty children and mean, uncaring adults. However, his books are often funny. In them some characters are smart and kind, and they make sure that good wins over evil. Scary or funny, Roald's stories are full of adventures that readers everywhere can enjoy.

"And what a palace it was! It had one hundred rooms, and everything was made of either dark or light chocolate! The bricks were chocolate, and the cement holding them together was chocolate, and all the walls and ceilings were made of chocolate, so were the carpets and the pictures and the furniture and the beds; and when you turned on the taps in the bathroom, hot chocolate came pouring out."

—From p. 13, Charlie and the Chocolate Factory

A South Wales Childhood

Roald was always very close to his mother, Sofie Dahl.

Roald Dahl was the son of Harald and Sofie Dahl. The Dahls were Norwegians who had settled in South Wales, a part of Great Britain. Roald was born on September 12, 1916, in the village of Llandaff.

Harald Dahl was a **widower** when he married Roald's mother. He already had a son and a daughter from his first marriage. In his writings Roald calls his half sister and half brother his "ancient sister" and "ancient brother." Roald was Harald and Sofie's third child and their only son. When Roald was three years old, his older sister, Astri, died of an illness. A few weeks later, his father, who was a wealthy businessman, died of **pneumonia**.

Roald started school when he was six. He went to a local school in Llandaff called Elmtree House. Six was also the age at which Roald learned how to tie his shoelaces!

Dear Mama
I hope you are quite well. I have just written this postcard to ask you, if you could send me a prayer book, but it must be the last one I had. I can not find it in church, please send it before sunday. love from boy

There were about 150 boys at St. Peter's when Roald went there. The arrow points to Roald, who is in the third row from the front. Inset: Every Sunday morning the students at St. Peter's would write to their families. In this letter Roald asks his mother to send him a new prayer book.

Boarding School

When Roald was nine, he went to St. Peter's School, a private **boarding school** for boys in Somerset, England. English boarding schools were believed to offer an excellent education. However, they were also places of strong **discipline**. Nearly all the students at St. Peter's were beaten, including Roald. A student could be beaten for eating in class or talking during study period. Years later the teachers and older students who treated Roald meanly were **inspirations** for the evil and unloving characters in the books he wrote for children. In 1988, Roald **published** *Matilda*. It was about a very smart girl and her adventures at school.

Roald's family spent summer vacations in Norway, his parents' native country. During the trips Roald loved to hear the Norwegian myths, or stories, his grandmother told. Witches and other characters from these myths appear in his books.

Into Africa

In 1929, when Roald was 13, he entered Repton Preparatory School in Derbyshire, England. During his final year, he decided he would rather go to work than attend college. He dreamed of working for a company that would send him to an exciting place, preferably Africa or China. At 18, Roald was hired by the Shell Company, which is an oil company. He earned five pounds a week, which was a good salary at the time. For two years Shell trained Roald to become a fuel salesman in a **tropical** country. In 1936, Shell decided to send Roald to East Africa. Jumping up and down at the news, Roald shouted, "Lions! And elephants and giraffes and coconuts everywhere."

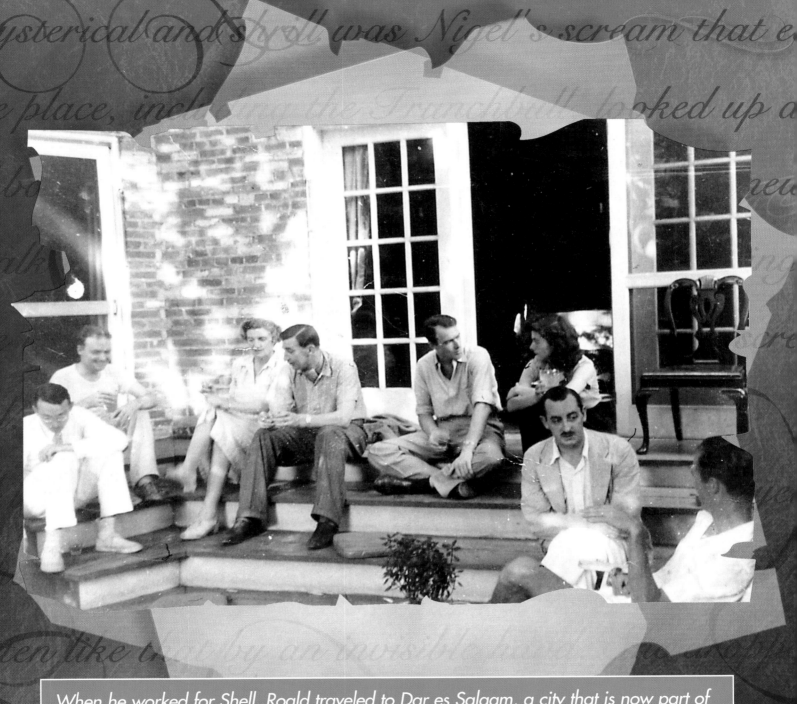

When he worked for Shell, Roald traveled to Dar es Salaam, a city that is now part of Tanzania in Africa. His job was selling oil to the Englishmen who were in charge of mines. Roald (center) lived in a big house with other salespeople.

During his training in Nairobi, Kenya, Roald's days were filled from 5:30 A.M. until 6:00 P.M. with flying and going to lessons.

The Beginning of a War

One day in 1939, Roald heard that England and other European countries were at war with Germany. It was the start of **World War II**. Roald left Shell and joined the Royal Air Force (RAF) in Nairobi, Kenya. For six months he and 15 other men trained to become fighter **pilots**. They learned to fly biplanes that had two sets of wings, two **cockpits**, and machine guns for shooting at other airplanes.

RAF officers were concerned that Roald, at 6 feet 6 inches (2 m), would be too tall for the cockpit. Roald was so set on becoming a pilot that he made himself fit by crunching himself up.

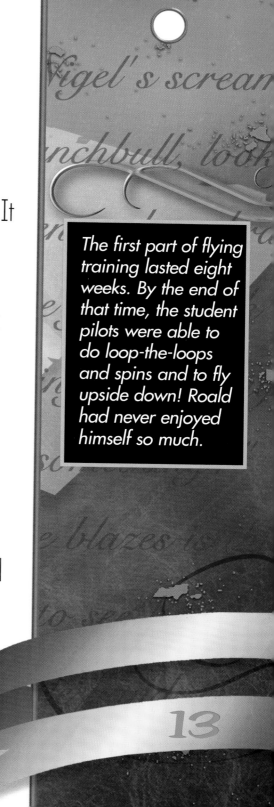

The first part of flying training lasted eight weeks. By the end of that time, the student pilots were able to do loop-the-loops and spins and to fly upside down! Roald had never enjoyed himself so much.

13

Crashing in the Desert

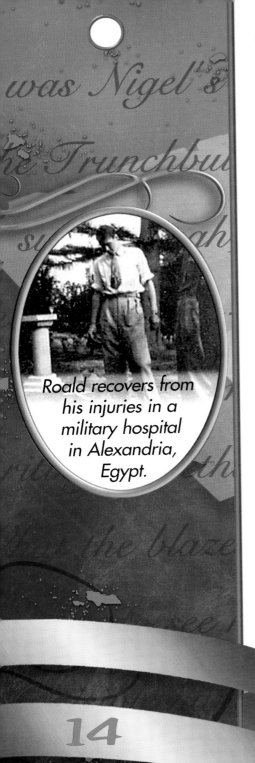

Roald recovers from his injuries in a military hospital in Alexandria, Egypt.

After training for six months, Roald was ordered to fly solo to Libya. He was to join a team of fighter pilots. Roald had had little experience flying long distances. It began to grow dark as he flew over a desert. He decided to look for a place to land so that he could continue the journey the next day. As he flew the plane lower, it hit a large rock and crashed. Fortunately, British soldiers found Roald and the destroyed plane. Roald was seriously **injured** and was blind for a short while. He spent many months healing. When he got well enough to fly, Roald was **eager** to rejoin the RAF. In 1941, he flew in many air battles against German fighter planes over Greece.

When he crashed in the desert, Roald was flying a Gloster Gladiator, shown here. Inset: In 1942, Roald wrote about the crash in the article "A Piece of Cake." The title was changed to "Shot Down Over Libya" to make it sound more exciting.

Roald started out writing for adults. After he became a father, however, Roald began to write for children. He thought it was harder to write for children, since he felt it was not easy to hold a child's attention.

The Writing Life

Roald had to quit flying in 1941 when he started to get bad headaches that affected his flying. A year later he found a job working for the British **Embassy** in Washington, D.C. While there he wrote his first magazine article, "Shot Down Over Libya," for the *Saturday Evening Post*. He was paid $1,000, a good sum of money in those days. In a short time, Roald was writing articles and short stories for popular magazines.

In 1943, Roald wrote his first book, *The Gremlins*. It is about evil creatures who cause many problems for RAF pilots during World War II. Two years later Roald moved back to England to be near his mother, who was not well. He continued to write his stories.

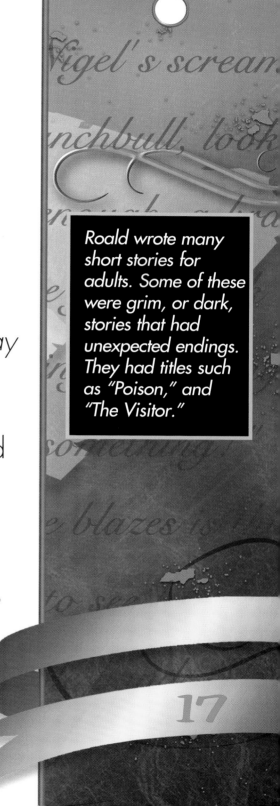

Roald wrote many short stories for adults. Some of these were grim, or dark, stories that had unexpected endings. They had titles such as "Poison," and "The Visitor."

Sad Events

"The news that a peach almost as big as a house had suddenly appeared in someone's garden had spread like wildfire across the countryside, and the next day a stream of people came scrambling up the steep hill to gaze upon this marvel."

—From p. 21, James and the Giant Peach

In 1953, Roald Dahl met and married American actress Patricia Neal. The couple bought a farmhouse in England where they raised five children. In 1960, their son Theo's stroller was hit by a taxicab when the family was visiting New York City. Although Theo lived he suffered injuries that left him **brain damaged**. In 1962, their oldest daughter, Olivia, died at the age of seven from an illness. Three years later Roald's wife Patricia suffered a stroke. Throughout this series of **tragedies**, Roald continued to write. He wrote one of his most popular children's books, *James and the Giant Peach*, in 1961.

For a while Patricia's stroke left her disabled and unable to speak. Roald helped nurse her back to health. Roald and Patricia are shown here with Theo and baby Ophelia at their home in Great Missenden, England.

ROALD DAHL

ILLUSTRATED BY QUENTIN BLAKE

Matilda

Matilda *is the story of a bright young girl. Matilda teaches herself to read at the age of three. By the time she is four, she is reading many of the books in her local library!*

Recognition and Awards

In 1983, Patricia and Roald **divorced**. Later that year Roald married Felicity Crosland. They lived on Roald's farm in Great Missenden where they raised animals. Until his death in 1990, Roald walked every day to a small brick building near the main farmhouse. This is where he went to write.

Roald has earned great recognition for his writing. Among many other **awards**, he was given the Whitbread Award. This is Britain's most important children's book award. Some people said that his books were too **crude** or **violent**. Roald replied that his books showed that children had the strength and skill to overcome the hardships that life presented to them.

"You are lying to me, madam!" the Trunchbull shouted, glaring at Matilda. *"I doubt there is a single child in the entire school who can read that book, and here you are, an unhatched shrimp sitting in the lowest form there is, trying to tell me a whopping lie like that!"*

—From p. 156, Matilda

In His Own Words

Sometimes it took Roald up to six months to write a story.

What is it like writing a book?

When you're writing it's rather like going on a very long walk, across valleys and mountains and things, and you get the first view of what you see and you write it down. Then you walk a bit further, maybe up on top of a hill, and you see something else, then you write that and you go on like that.

How do you get the ideas for your stories?

It starts always with a tiny little seed of an idea . . . and that even doesn't come very easily. You can be mooching around for a year or so before you get a good one. When I do get a good one, mind you, I quickly write it down so that I won't forget it.

What is your work routine?

My work routine is very simple and it's always been so for the last 45 years. The great thing, of course, is never to work too long at a stretch because after about 2 hours you are not at your highest peak of concentration. . . . I start at 10 o'clock and I stop at 12. Always.

What is the secret to keeping your readers entertained?

My lucky thing is I laugh at exactly the same jokes that children laugh at and that's one of the reasons I'm able to do it.

Glossary

awards (uh-WORDZ) Things that are given after careful thought.

boarding school (BOR-ding SKOOL) A school where students live during the school year.

cockpits (KOK-pits) The places in airplanes where the pilots sit.

crude (KROOD) Lacking in good manners or taste.

damaged (DA-mijd) Harmed as a result of an illness or accident.

discipline (DIH-sih-plin) Training by teaching and exercise.

divorced (dih-VORST) Ended a marriage legally.

eager (EE-guhr) Excited about something.

embassy (EM-buh-see) An official office of a country's representatives.

injured (IN-jurd) Harmed or hurt.

inspirations (in-spuh-RAY-shunz) Powerful, moving guidance.

pilots (PY-luts) People who fly aircraft or spacecraft.

pneumonia (noo-MOHN-ya) An illness that people can get in their lungs.

published (PUH-blishd) Printed so that people can read it.

tragedies (TRA-jeh-deez) Very sad events.

tropical (TRAH-puh-kul) Warm year-round.

widower (WIH-doh-er) A man whose wife has died.

World War II (WURLD WOR TOO) A war fought by the United States, Great Britain, France, and the Soviet Union against Germany, Japan, and Italy from 1939 to 1945.

violent (VY-lent) Marked by strong, rough force.

Index

Web Sites

Due to the changing nature of Internet links, PowerKids Press has
developed an online list of Web sites related to the subject of this book.
This site is updated regularly. Please use this link to access the list:
www.powerkidslinks.com/aa/roaldahl/